MEDITATIONS AND POEMS FROM A YEAR

UNDER THE OAK

NATALIE FÉE

With wild love!

Natalie x

Under the Oak

For

Jack o' the Hill

Contents

Introduction

At dawn on the winter solstice of 2023, I climbed the hill behind my house, into the woods, up to the solitary oak tree in the meadow and sat down at its trunk. Facing the rising sun, although it was probably cloudy that day, I set out my intention to visit this same spot for the next 365 days: until the next winter solstice. No holidays, no spontaneous family visits, no work trips. I'd be rooted here, in my hometown, making a daily pilgrimage to the oak.

Most people thought I was mad to embark on such a commitment, which also involved filming the tree, so that at the end of the year, I (or a more capable filmmaker) might be able to stitch it all together and create a visual journey of the oak's four seasons. My family rolled their eyes and accepted this as another one of my weird and wonderful experiments – even though I'd never done anything like it before. My friends were curious. One or two thought it was a lovely idea. I knew people would think it strange, but overall, their levels of resistance to the project took me by surprise. I even made a list of people's 'reasons not to do it / how to make it easier'[1] as I was readying myself to begin the year. I, however, was certain I needed to do it, for reasons that will hopefully reveal themselves to you in these poems.

I had no idea if I'd be physically able to visit the oak every single day; life has a habit of throwing curveballs, and with ageing parents and a son living on the other side of the planet, my best laid plans could very easily go awry. My work was flexible at the time – as the founder of an environmental campaigning group with a CEO in charge of the day-to-day running of the organisation I was mostly working from home and only required to travel from time to time. I was also a busy keynote speaker, but speaking abroad was only occasional and I reckoned I could turn the odd job down should I need to. My record label, who I was working with on my debut album at the time, were supportive, agreeing to work with me across single days in the studio in London instead of a week at a time. On those days, I'd go to the tree as early as 5.45am, meditate for 20 minutes, then jump in the car and get on the motorway.

It was a big commitment, and there were most definitely days throughout the year when I questioned why I was doing it. My husband and friends were very supportive – coming with me on days when a work commitment meant it had gotten too dark for me to feel safe going on my own. Wild winter storms of various names came and went, exciting invitations declined, yet – and I'll always look back on this as some kind of magic – nothing stopped me. It was as if (and of course I'd prayed many times for it to be so) my commitment had a protective spell over it. That's not to say I didn't encounter many challenges throughout the year, one of which knocked me for six, but I didn't get sick, nobody around me had an emergency, and the oak and I were able to spend every day of that year together.

Quite soon into my daily visits to the oak, I realised that as well as filming and photography, I wanted to journal, and decided it would be a good idea to write a poem a day. Partly as a way to document the year, but also as a way to ground the experience – to transmute it from energy into form. The daily poems became an important and mostly joyful part of the process, however I had unintentionally added a whole other layer of commitment to what was already a big challenge, and some nights I'd find myself at 11.30pm sitting at my laptop trying to write or finish a poem before midnight. Then, one lazy, sunny day in July, under the oak, I noticed something. The meadow was resting. The oak was resting. But I wasn't. All the quiet survival and inner work of Winter, followed by the momentous, dynamic happening of Spring, was followed by this lovely lull of late Summer. The growing had peaked, the flowering was done and the energy all around me was one of simple, total ease. I knew that day I was pushing myself too hard with the daily poems, and needed to do what nature was doing ... take a break. So I did. From mid-July onwards I wrote when I felt like it, not because I had to. The selection of poems in this book span all four seasons, and possibly reflect (in terms of volume) the energy of the season and how much I was writing – Winter is reflective, sparse and somewhat serious, Spring and Summer are a total riot and Autumn conveys the harvest, the dying back, and possibly the early spores of fermentation.

On the topic of seasons, in oak time, assuming she[2] lives to be 400 years old, a year of my life is the equivalent of a single season of hers. So one of 1,600, as opposed to one of my 80, if I live that long. I do wonder though, if the ring in her trunk that year might appear different to the others. Imbued with the colours of our daily communions and everything held in these poems.

Then there was the meadow, and the winding path itself – the unexpected allies of this journey. As you'll read (if you do start from the beginning, in Winter), the joy of witnessing the transformation of an unassuming field of short grass into an explosion of buzzing life and colour reaching over my head was utterly, profoundly glorious. And there I was thinking it was all about the oak.

I hope you'll be able to receive some of this energy through these words, and maybe even be encouraged to begin, or deepen your relationship with your local patch of wild and our shared plant friends. If I had to whittle down my experience into a spoon made of oak, and could bring just one mouthful to your lips, it would be this: nature is rooting for you, it knows exactly what you need, and is always, always at the ready to offer it. You just need to be still enough to receive it.

1. Reasons not to do it / how to make it easier (genuine suggestions made by other people):

- You could make a cardboard cut-out and leave it there
- Angus (my husband) can dress up as you and go some days instead of you
- Why don't you just edit yourself into the shot in post-production?
- For God's sake why not do it when you're 80?
- What about your husband?
- Why not take a branch home with you?
- You could take a baby oak tree around with you in a pot
- Why not sit under a different oak tree?

2. Throughout this book you may see me referring to the oak using 'she/her' pronouns. This is based on my perception of the essence, or consciousness, of this particular tree as feminine.

WINTER

the land has emptied itself of doing
withdrawn, at rest, in stillness.

what happens
when I live like this?

leaning into a wintering oak
all of me gathered under its naked boughs

until this new way of being
takes root, shoots and breathes

I sit under a tree.

come, sit, breathe
the trees can show us how it's done –
how to root in uncertain times
how to slow down
and how to rest

sometimes, the right tree
can show us something else;
how to hear the song in our heart
and how to sing it to the wind
so the world can dance.

mind resists the rain
not body
when body is warm and covered
rain is a gift to receive

just listen to robin and blackbird sing
they know a thing or two about the weather.

wind knocks me sideways
each gust blowing away my concentration

I try to focus on my breath again
while I'm being blown around
hair in my face, body buffeted,
I send down roots, I practice going deeper within
to be still, even when the storm is raging.

i sit
i breathe
i open
i sit
i breathe
i am.

how can a tree, all bark and bud
slumbering in its winter
hold at its core a light so golden
it makes a mirror of the sun?

if I sit here long enough, still enough
do I rediscover my nature?
if I come here every day, open
do the cycles start to speak through me again?

will I remember a time, far back in my bones
when I was once one with land and sky?

sitting here each morning
in the cold, bright stillness of dawn
I realise my mind has been expecting
wondering what's happening
anticipating an experience

but today I heard the words
perhaps whispered on the crystalline air
winter is patient

it goes against the modern ways
the habit of always doing
and here, the oak is my invitation
to simply be with it
while it winters.

does a tiger get tired waiting to pounce?
or a heron waiting for the perfect fish?
I doubt it.

they are masters of readiness;
poised
focused
relaxed

I am a novice in such ways
so am practising on a tree
as, unlike most things,
it can't run away.

some days if I feel a little unwieldy
unsettled, unfocused, uncomfortable
I remember my feet
and place them on the soil

rooting, grounding
planting, tending

trees know how to do this
growing down as they grow up
making friends with the earth
while they play with the stars.

beginning again
starting with emptiness
waiting to be moved
this way or that
but always towards
what is opening
always towards
what is yes
and always inching closer
to you.

a prophet, a buddha, a mystic
all had a thing about 40 days
but today is just another day
for me and the tree

birds fly in, dog runs by
wind whistles through
woman sits down.

the land is stirring
yet not quite awake

except for the early risers
like the snowdrop

she likes to be up before the others
to have the woods to herself a while

she knows how happy we are to see her
and how gladly we drink her medicine

our wintered hands that long for warmth
our weathered souls seeking signs of life

snowdrop's joy is in ours
as she flowers on the quiet cusp of spring.

walk into the misty wilds
and sit timeless for a while
feel the cool shroud of grey
welcome you into the quiet

here, in the space between breaths
all prayers are answered

walk into the misty wilds
and sit timeless for a while
stillness is waiting for you to know
this peace within your heart.

where do we go when we just don't know?
to the trees, we go to the trees
to rest, to dream, to see the unseen
to the trees, we go to the trees.

of all the people I meet on the hill
only one other comes alone

the rest think they're in service
to their four-legged friends
who race like blurry balls of energy
across the fields and through the woods

the trees know it's the other way around
and have their own fond name for dogs:
'bringers of people
out of their homes'.

drip drip drip
awareness falls like rain from above
all we have to do to receive it
is be willing to get wet from time to time

some days a trickle
others a downpour
the heart is a vessel
waiting to be filled.

sometimes I come to you
with a mind full of stuff
an inability to hear
the stillness of my heart

on these days it seems
neither the birdsong
nor the rarest of blue skies
can compete for my attention

but you don't mind
as you've seen it all before
how sometimes the ivy grows so thick
you might forget you're an oak

you understand the way of things
why some days I can't sit still
so you keep on calling my name
to remind me who I am.

sit a while and notice
how under my outstretched branches
you are held in a perfect sphere
as above, so below
as you come, so we grow

today the storm was within
when outside was relatively calm
trying to find stillness on days like these
can feel like trying to tether the wind

maybe some days we just have to wait it out
until the sun comes out from behind the clouds
and we see what hidden treasure
has washed up on the shore.

be like a bud, warming yourself in the winter sun
something inside you is waking up
moving from the depths of winter
into the welcoming arms of the spring

there's no rush in this space
no hurry to greet the light
just a gentle remembering
of the wonder of change.

SPRING

softening the edges
of the dark, cold hedges
the mother of the wood does bloom

gentle and fierce
careless hands she may pierce
if she's not given ample room

blackthorn the bringer
oh the spring song singer
carry us from winter's gloom!

today I slipped out of my skin
out of my mind
and for while I was free

layers unzipped, undone
fell from my shoulders
in a heap

no big song and dance
no cosmic fandango
and yet there I am

another version of me
resting in the stillness
beyond the veil.

welcome little yellow ones
opening your petals
to dance with the wind

I wonder if the oak
is as glad to see you
as I am?

now we are three –
the narcissus, the tree
and me.

all around me life is unfurling
seeds shooting
shoots spiralling
a collective movement up from the soil

we're all just lifting ourselves
day by day towards the sky
united in our love
for the stars.

part of me isn't ready for spring
for the coming rush and burst of green
I stopped to listen to her –

she had quite a lot to say.

what if I was patient with myself
as winter is with spring?
no pressure or hurry
just a quiet trust
in the nature of things
to flower in their own sweet time

I think more of me would be at peace
resting in the knowing that flowering
– like the spring –
is not a matter of 'if'
but 'when'.

there once was a tree-hugging missus
who was rather fond of narcissus
she rejoiced in their flowers
(thought they had special powers)
and bent o'er to give 'em all kissus!

we did not come here to mourn
all that is beyond our control

or to make our hearts carry
the weight of winter into the spring

we came to discover what makes
our soul shine

and how we can, with these god-given hands
weave a little more light into the world

that's what a shooting star is ...
a worry dissolving
into grace.

take me away from the machines
from the ever-scrolling screens
and into the deep green wood

where the stag is my king
and the feathered ones sing
in praise of the wild and the good.

I'll sit with you in the morning dew
'neath branches bare and brown
and pray our cup is filled right up
from roots unto the crown.

do not worry about being alone
in this world

instead, sit quietly under a tree
and listen

after a while you will remember
to whom you have always belonged.

so tender is a green shoot
see how easily it can be broken

anything new is like that
we open ourselves to the world
and risk something being crushed

yet it always find a way
to grow back, braver.

come, beloved, come
the trees are calling to you
offering sweet sanctuary
for your world-weary soul

come, beloved, come
the trees want you to know
they will happily fill your heart
as well as your lungs.

I sit with you in the morning sun
giving thanks for all you bring
I watch your garden come alive
rising up to greet the spring

I sit with you in pouring rain
giving thanks for all you water
I feel you kiss you my cheek and say
it's good to see you, daughter.

this morning I wondered
if the birds are calling in the spring
lifting the green shoots from the earth
with their song

imagine that

if it were true there would be no spring
unless the feathered ones were here
to sing it in.

my busy, wandering mind
seems to be even louder
here in the peace of the oak

is the silence amplifying
what's already there
or is the oak stirring the pot?

some mornings my mind bores me to tears
they run silently down my cheeks
and fall on the patient earth.

we feel hurt
we blame someone
for making us feel bad

we feel hurt
we tend to the pain
and ask it what it needs

we feel hurt
we thank spirit
for showing us our wounds

life loves us that way
always sending us what we need
to grow, to heal, to fly.

grass kenning

wind-dancer
water-keeper
soil-stitcher
shelter-giver
tree-hugger
cricket-lover
dew-dropper
show-stopper.

there's a spirit in everything
that speaks to those who listen

some hearts are like a bud shut tight
guarded and vigilant against the frost
remembering all the times they opened
to the cold shoulder of winter

to those hearts nature calls –
bring me your pain to heal
come home to my arms and I'll carry you
into the sweet warmth of spring.

nature doesn't care for
who you think you are
where you call home
or what you're into

the healing is free
the clinic always open
a tonic for body and soul
forever on prescription

so come one, come all
into the arms of the wild
and let's drink the medicine
made for these times.

all hail the tiny blooms
of forget-me-not returning
inviting a sweet remembrance
that you too carry a star
in your heart

she is singing:
forget-you-not
the light that you are
see how the sun at your centre
lights up the whole blue sky!

it's ok to look away
to close your eyes for a while
and seek solace in the silence

the humanness of this world
is sometimes too much
for our loving hearts to bear

there will always be those
that have yet to see
we are all related.

next time you're with a tree
that seems to call to your heart
sit with it a while and ask
'what do you need?'

although the answer may not come
in a language you understand
or in a day, a moon or season
it will always be glad that you asked.

balanced now are night and day
under this tree I see the way

roots as deep as branches high
holding just as much earth as she does sky.

there is peace here under the tree
on the hill
there are places like this we can go
to feel the peace already in us
they want us to come
so we can remember
this peace
and be filled
so filled
that we start spilling over
and splashing everyone we meet.

when you sense the coming storm
don't stiffen

see how the grass yields
the daffodils dance
and the tall trees sing it through

they know of its great power
to show us where we are still vulnerable
so we can gently tend to those parts
when it passes.

the narcissus have gone, for now
they came, they flowered, they faded

I waited so long for them to arrive
for their sunny faces to light up my mornings

now the golden yellows have turned to brown
and the green will return to its bulbs

that show was fifty weeks in the making
for two weeks of joyful dancing

I'm so glad that this year
I had a front row seat.

don't do nothing
do something

even tiny acts matter
when they come from our heart

serving those who need us
winged, finned, four-legged or two

is the way to peace

but don't act from guilt
or shame

this world doesn't need more pain
or for us to suffer

it only needs us to open
just a little more to this love.

this morning my heart was singing
'thank-you, thank-you, thank-you!'
for nothing in particular
and everything at once

then so quickly on its heels came the thought
'is it ok to feel happy when others are not?'

perhaps this is the way of things;
beyond all talk of right and wrong
our heart knows how deeply we are loved
and can't quite believe its luck.

surely a dewdrop
shimmering in the morning sun
knows a thing or two
about why we are here

see the way it winks at you?

it wants you to know its secret

how to turn this invisible light
into all the colours of the world.

every morning these days
a different flower appears in the meadow –
many of whose names I've yet to learn

it's a bit like the oak and I
have been getting ready for a party
and now the guests are starting to arrive

or maybe it's the other way around;
they've been here all along
and it's me who's finally showed up.

thanks for the poems
I said to the tree
at the very same time
that she said it to me

I don't think I was dreaming
for it felt clear as the sky
that we spoke with one voice
the old oak tree and I.

every act
in service of this great love
flies like a burning arrow of grace
into the heart of the world

it is not lost there
but for a time cannot be seen
while it gathers its light

we cannot know where it will land
only that it was right to send it
and trust, at the end of the day
it was enough.

the thought crossed my mind today
'what if I'm sitting on buried treasure
like in the storybooks?'

I laughed!

I've already found
so many precious jewels
in this tiny meadow
under this humble tree
beneath this welcoming sky

just keep digging deeper
my love, they all said
there is so much more
yet to discover.

the bud and the bee
on the branch of the tree
danced on this windy morning

I prayed to the tree
for my heart to fly free
on the wings of the new day dawning.

all is quickening now
the soft grass in the meadow
the bursting buds of trees
all is returning to the light

all is quickening now
the quiet flowering in our hearts
the longing just to love one another
all is returning to the light.

you're changing before my eyes
your buds are bursting
but not loudly

day by day you open
just a little more
and something soft emerges

green, tender, fresh
new but known
as you've done this
a hundred times before –
or more

like a soul remembering
in its mortal body
who it came here to be.

please wait a year
I am installing updates from the meadow
downloads from the tree
anti-virus programmes from the sweet spring air
and a new operating system from the daily ritual
of coming here

wait! am I connected to a power source?

always, replied the sun as it kissed my face this morning.

even though on the surface of things
in spring
nature seems to be in a hurry
a rush of opening buds
a race of the lush green grass
towards the sky

the deep work, the slow steady kind
of thickening bark and deepening roots
is invisible to the eye

that kind of change takes patience
stretching out over many moons
many seasons and for some
many lifetimes

this is what she is teaching me:
a few hundred bulbs planted in winter
does not a bluebell wood make come spring.

half an hour of each day
dedicated to quietening
settling, stilling

is such a tease!

I'm sure the trees, hills
sea and stars
would love me to stay

to listen to them for longer
to go deeper and deeper
into this mostly unseen world

where everything, everything
is alive.

I come to the tree full
in the hope I might become empty
not in a sad, lonely way
empty of all joy

but hollow
in the hope I might become an instrument
for the wild wood to sing through
and make of my life a song.

(forget-me-nots)

we want another poem, they said
with the voice of a thousand stars
glittering blue and yellow

we want you to tell them, they said
how to open to our brilliance
so their hearts may be happy

we want you to remember, they said
when we fade back into darkened soil
our light is forever yours to shine!

clarity comes like a late spring breeze
helping us see the wood for the trees
the clouds finally lift and the mind agrees
for the heart to return to a place of ease.

SUMMER

meadow rising
leaves unfurling
sky bluing
birds returning

dogs chasing
owners meeting
woman sitting
sunshine seeking

sweet smelling
breeze blowing
eyes shining
heart glowing.

when we walk into nature –
or skip or dream or dance or fly
we often meet that wild part of ourselves
the part that feels at home again
the part that remembers the only rules
are to love as best we can
the land upon which we find our feet
and the ones we walk on it with.

today the buttercups arrived
they definitely weren't here yesterday
but have clearly had a busy night
orchestrating their arrival
a synchronised opening
a flourish of togetherness
in the meadow
at dawn

I wonder if we humans could do this
if, gathered under the stars one night
we could remind each other to awaken
and – united in our flowering –
make the world even more beautiful
than it already is.

a most auspicious morning
oh what blessing did descend
a divinely juicy dropping
from my little feathered friend

great fortune now awaits me
for I am the lucky one
my body now anointed
with the contents of their bum.

some days the softness of the grass
seems like it could heal all ills
if only we'd lay down more often
on its green velvet blanket
and be reminded how to live
as if we cared and loved
every blade
every feather
every bone
as our own.

every morning I'm bathed in the song
of the winged ones
and I give thanks
for how it makes me feel –
for the easing of my shoulders
for the rooting of my feet
for the rising in my chest

all this because of them
the wild chorus of the woods
without whom this land
(and I)
would be lost.

"is she real?"
I heard a child say this morning
her voice falling like a feather
into the field of my awareness

I don't know how long I'd been sitting
or how long she'd been watching
but soon my whole being was laughing
and she saw I was real, and I was happy.

what is a pilgrim?
is it a person who moves –
in some way, with intention –
away from what's known
towards that which is still a mystery?

what is a pilgrimage?
is it the soul's journey
following the winding path
of the heart's ascent?

it feels a bit like that
when I climb the hill each day
and sit under the oak

and I wonder, in my coming here
if each day my spirit moves –
in some tiny, immeasurable way –
towards the sky.

today I only had ears for the swifts
screaming into the skies above me
we're back! they called
what news?

well, I said
not much, except
this year I'm here to greet you
more fully than ever before

this year I was waiting
for your riotous return
carrying the summer on your wings
singing it in with your song

this year I was alive
to the joy of your homecoming
and felt summer land in my heart
while you sky-danced over the hill.

the may bug came to remind me
of how short one life can be
and how we can spend most of it in the dark
not knowing who we're destined to become

I want the smell of this summer morning
to linger in my nose forever
to be able to draw great lungfuls
of thick blossom air into my body
every day like this

I inhale and remember –
if only for one deep breath –
all that is sweet in the world.

my beloved tree friend
is now in the business
of making shade
the sun at its height
casting a perfect circle
within which I sit

today the light
dappled on my brow
as if it was working
together with the leaves
to ease the sorry frown
I'd brought with me.

may I be available
to receive
the gift that's here
just waiting for me
to open to it

may I be present
to notice
the infinite number of offerings
held out to me
in each and every moment

may I make of my life
a grateful prayer
that I am starting to know
and love
the spirit in all things.

only the wind can turn a meadow
into a rolling sea of green waves

today the oak
was my ship

and for a moment we were sailing
on top of the hill.

since the coming of warmth
all has been opening
each day a new arrival

another part of the whole
starts to bloom
and offers itself to the world

some days it seems
I can feel my heart
remembering how to do that

guided by the opening
of flowers.

the meadow has come alive
jumping things and crawling things
flying things and buzzing things

and I hear in this sweet surge of life
a joyful song of knowing:
the birds will have food
the plants will get pollinated

all is not lost.

bugs can be thugs
a real distraction
my ankles and arms
the main attraction.

can you sometimes hear the language of trees?
the wise fluttering that speaks through a thousand leaves
the soft muttering carried on a gentle breeze

you do?
me too.

I thought I was here for the silence
a rest for my ears, my mind
from the noise

but then a bird shares a new song
and the wind starts playing the leaves
and a bumble bee hums along

then I realise it's not silence that I come for,
but peace.

I'm finally starting to see results
from all this meditation
today I even found myself
engaged in levitation

a mouse came scuttling through the grass
it gave me such a scare
that without the slightest effort
I was three feet in the air.

remember when we were just three
the narcissus, myself and the tree?
turns out the rest were asleep
but now they've sprung up from the deep
and here in the meadow we're plenty
at the last count I reached more than twenty

cow parsley, wild fennel and buttercups
forget-me-nots still hanging on
daisies, iris and nettles,
cleavers and red campion

red dock, yarrow and plantain
dandelions going to seed
herb robert, white archangel
ground ivy and hawkweed

meadow cranesbill, cuckoo flower
all the sweet and velvet grasses
have all become my dearest friends
until the summer passes.

weeds are wild
and wild is good
and good are the weeds
that wild the wood.

I came to the tree feeling broken today
perhaps expecting some kind of healing –
a loving embrace on the breeze
a sign that I won't have to experience that again
please, not again
but the only kind I got was a firm nudge
back down the hill
to help somebody else

these are some things trees can remind us of
how to stay available
how to stay open
how to serve
even when our heart aches –
especially when our heart aches.

sometimes, when I speak to the plants from my heart
(which will usually involve a thank-you)
I feel the same words coming back to me, in unison
as if they know exactly what I'm about to say
and want me to hear it too

in that moment we are one
both giver and receiver of love.

june arrives, full of warmth and colour
her days long as the grass

the land greets her with flowers
the swifts sing her favourite song

if I could make you a month
I'd choose june

so you can know what it is
to show up in the world like that
and receive such a blessed welcome.

daisy, daisy, give me your answer do
the secrets of the universe
are held inside of you

the pattern of creation
emblazoned on your heart
as you spiral into being
nature's perfect work of art.

enter into the dew-soaked fields
before the wind and sun have reclaimed them

enter into the sweet smelling soft
of the meadow's morning welcome

enter into the peace
of the land that waits to greet you
that already knows your name

enter into your heart
where love grows
wild as weeds.

I am noticing so much more
in me, in you, in the meadow
there are so many layers of deepening
so many levels of awareness
I don't think it ever stops
and I wonder
how much more present can I be
to the arrival of summer
to the needs of someone I love
to the aliveness of the spirit in my heart?

to me a summer playlist has become
something else altogether

the changing music of the oak leaves –
fresh green, softly whispering
only weeks ago
and now they rustle, crisp and brisk\

the sound of the long grasses
inching up each day to sway
their shushing, rubbing
whistling in the breeze

the call of the swifts
joyous screaming
communal shrieking
blessing dawn and dusk

the song in my heart
becoming easier to hear
is that because I am listening more
or has she learned to sing in harmony with the seasons?

the later that I climb the hill
the more the dogs increase
which I'm not sure is conducive
to finding inner peace

some are nonchalant and mellow
have a sniff and off they go
others are more boisterous
and put on quite a show

there are those that like to lick my face
one particular alsatian
who seems to think he has the right
to interrupt my meditation.

the oak and the daisies
danced in the air
while the wind kissed my cheeks
and tousled my hair.

the beetle – part one

today the sun was shining
the wind had stopped its blowing
so I decided to be bold
and climb the hill with my legs showing

underneath the oak I sat
quietening my mind
when a beetle said 'you're in the way'
and pincered my behind

I carried on, I doubled down
these bare limbs won't stop me yet
but then the itching started
and my resolve became regret

flying, jumping, crawling things
every blade of grass a tickle
the meadow that I've grown so fond of
now one giant spiky prickle

if you like to meditate outside
I'll leave you with these thoughts
stillness is elusive
especially in shoughts.

the beetle – part two (the next day)

today beetle came back for more
but I was well equipped
as today I wore my leggings
so my behind remained unnipped.

golden was the light
on that summer solstice morning
golden were our hearts
with the spirit in us dawning

the tree abides in deep peace
I visit to remember the part of me
that does too.

each day I renew my commitment
to open to this world

and each day the world offers
a thousand ways
to do it.

the meadow has grown very tall
in fact as tall as I
that doesn't mean I'm very small
just that the grass is high.

today the grasshoppers hatched
in one glorious act of togetherness
and now the meadow sings its summer song

how did that happen?
how does an entire choir assemble overnight?
perhaps the sun whispered in their ears and said
now my loves, now

it whispers in mine
but unlike the grasshopper
and most others here
my flowering seems not to be
an overnight phenomenon
but a slow and steady opening
to its light.

the meadow is turning
green to gold
dried, dyed
and very much july'd.

from within the heart of stillness
a gentle grace did spring
and for while I saw the light
I saw the light in everything

I waited a long time to meet you
not knowing your name
or who you were destined to be
when you flowered

don't step there
I told others
I'm waiting for my friend
to open

then you did
a thousand times over
illuminating the whole meadow
with your dancing orbs of light

now I'm greeted daily
with the sweetness of friendship
we bow to each other in the wind
the woman and the wild carrot.

yesterday on the hill I overheard a visitor
loudly declare to her friend
they should just cut down all these trees
so we can see the view

the trees and I let out a sigh

oh what a long way humans have to go
to remember our place in this world.

I remember you
as I enter the sacred stream
the stillness that carries
your love to me
and back into the world

is this how we tend
to the garden?
becoming so still
we gather as clouds
and start to rain holy droplets
onto all the beloved's flowers.

when is an oak's birthday?
is it the day it first fell from its mother
onto the earth as an acorn?
is it the day it was buried
by squirrel or jay?
or is it the day when the waters
of sky and soil united
to activate its awakening?

I don't know how old this oak is
but today was the day
the crickets and I sang out
happy birthday
perhaps for the first time
in its long, wild life.

it seems the fennel is last to flower
the others came and went
apart from dear wild carrot that is
with whom july I've mostly spent.

be still and let love enter
be still and let love through
be still and love will show you
the next one thing to do.

some passers-by
don't see that I'm here
and stand loudly talking
with a phone by their ear

what's that? paella?
yes I'll send you the recipe
oh thank-you, that's kind
yes I think it's my specialty

when is the funeral?
was it that terrible cough?
yes isn't it awful
oh wait the dog has run off

yes we're all packed up
just the kitchen to do
no thanks we've got help
but that's lovely of you

these are all but snippets
of phone calls I've heard
maybe I'll hang a sign
that says 'do not disturb'.

to some passers-by
I'm invisible to the eye
is it that the grass is as tall as me
or is it that I've now become one with the tree?

I thought they'd left unceremoniously
the skies suddenly quiet in their absence
and then I remembered
that soft summer evening
pink skies and a salty breeze
when they gathered
too many to count
more than I've seen at once

a party of swifts
darting, diving, screaming
dancing, dipping, weaving

and now I see
that was the last hurrah
heeding the call of the changing season

my heart soared with them then
and although I didn't know
it was their leaving party
I'm so very glad I was a guest
at the last wild dance of the summer.

the summer has peaked
swifts gone from the sky
the meadow is resting
and so am I.

what if our hearts
could see more of the sky
and what if they sang
until all the world cried
and all of those tears
rolled into the sea
what holy water that would be.

the meadow is turning to seed
and I too surrender to the process
quietening, strengthening
ripening in the summer sun.

she bade me kiss the acorn
the only one of the season
I asked her what would come of it
but she didn't give a reason.

the swifts have left
the sky bereft
for it loves to hear them sing

their summer song –
not sung for long –
now gone until the spring.

the poo on the path's turned purple
a seasonal gift to remind us
that when blackberry and elder are eaten
the summer will soon be behind us!

healing comes in many ways;

a pebble on the path
a feather in the grass
a sting from a nettle
or a bite on the arse.

although it looks as though
the flowers are contracting
curling themselves up into balls
retreating from the world

they are quietly at their most potent

surrendering their seed
to the wind, to the earth
to the birds, to my cardigan

an offering of wild hope
that we'll sow more love in this world.

(when will the crickets stop singing)

where will my little choir friends hop
when our beloved meadow gets the chop?

with their eggs safely laid
protected from blade
will the songs that they sang
simply stop?

AUTUMN

nature is rooting for you
the flower, the birdsong, the fallen leaf
are all offerings
each one a little parcel
of divine longing
just waiting for you to open.

be like a tree –
draw what inspires you down from the stars
draw what feeds you up from the earth
then, in that place in the middle where they meet
in that magical melding of sky and soil
put down your roots, open your arms
and quietly serve the whole world
with each and every breath.

the dark, quiet woods
sometimes need our attention
even more than the flowers
that were so very easy to love

there is a landscape within us
longing to be known so intimately
that we simply know, each morning
what part needs tending to today.

some days are deep days
some days are shallow days
some days are busy days
some days are fallow days

in time I'm learning not to care –
and trust my being here is the prayer.

she's not in a hurry to drop her leaves
anyone would think it still summer

we watched the ash turn first
right up until the last leaf

while the oak held
me tight.

it's happening more often now
I say something to the tree
—or the meadow or the sky—
and it responds in unison
our two voices as one
a reciprocal admission of love

I could be imagining it of course
but then again
what if I've been imagining all this time
that we were ever apart?

a tree can be our church
a meeting place of earth and sky
a quiet space to pray

the birds can be our choir
a moss-green stone for an altar
– the nature worship way.

this year's cricket meadow choir
are all officially dead
(there's no need
to pretend otherwise)

we give thanks for a wonderful season
(perhaps their most memorable run)

and of course special praise
must go to the last soloist
who could be heard trilling its sweet song
into the furthest reaches of autumn.

last week I heard one
this week I heard none.

the first easterly of the season
rattled and jangled my bones

it wasn't an unpleasant feeling
but my associations made it so

a bit like the police
showing up unannounced saying

the party is over kids
it's time to turn the music off.

(oaku)

oak is browning now
taking her sweet time to drop
while I learn to fall

I am not sorry for not being
who you want me to be
I am but a soul, travelling home
and my choices are mine
and mine alone

I will not bow to you
for my spirit has awoken
I am strong as the oak tree
and through these words
the spell is broken.

the oak knows my heart
better than I

she sees it all;
the longing, the potential
the unburdened light

like the calling in the acorn
she guides me to discover
who I am.

I watched you bud
I watched you spread
I watched you drop
your leaves now dead

but out of these
I now can find
a warming cushion
for my behind.

we call it death
but really it's a continuum
the seeds are activated
the buds are already on the branch
even as the leaves fall.

the loudest voice today was the wind's
howling, whistling, roaring
the storm shouting in my ears
I AM HERE!

I sat beneath the oak
blustered, buffeted, awed
my spirit soaring up from my chest
I AM HERE!

as the groves turn to concrete
as our gaze turns away from the stars
some forget how connected we were

how we spoke to the trees
seeking their counsel
invoking their blessings
enlisting their support

how we listened to the trees
opening to their wisdom
giving thanks for their guidance
accepting their love

some still remember
how we communed with the trees
and are kindling the sacred
for us all.

she
noticed
a little death
pulling her down
asking her to give it up
to drop her leaves and stand
naked in the truth of who she is.

a palette of brown and yellow and gold
notes of compost and mushroom and mould
this is the harvest wine we are tending
when all has fermented, cheers to the ending.

I used to ask my hidden parts
to tell me what they need
but lately, since I've found myself
at home amongst the trees
since the shafts of light
on the woodland path
and all the songbirds of the meadow
keep offering themselves
so readily to me each morning
they are in need of very little
and can only speak
of joy.

I praise the sky, I praise the land
I praise the soil on which I stand
I praise the rivers, I praise the trees
I praise the ever-rolling seas
I praise the moon, I praise the sun
I praise the air that fills my lungs
I praise the dark, I praise the light
I praise each day and praise each night
I praise the silence, praise the song
I praise this earth where I belong.

you all gathered on this day
to sing out my name
new to my ears
but known to my heart

I thought perhaps
it was the oak's
but no, so much of her
remains a mystery

even after a year
there are still
infinite jewels
to discover

shall we
begin again?

the sun, suspended
this journey, ended.

Acknowledgments

My thanks go first and foremost to my husband, Angus Barr, for accepting me for who I am – a wife that does crazy, some might say selfish things, like deciding to sit under a tree for a year. Thank you for supporting me despite not understanding it, and all the days (and nights!) you came with me when I needed you. I couldn't have done it without you. To my son, Elliot, for his tree knowledge and endless encouragement. To my mum, for being brave enough to listen, heal and move on. To the rest of my family for loving me as I am, for not getting sick that year and for being curious. To the dogwalkers who would stop to talk (if I had my eyes open). To Ted Waters and the eagle for the difficult days and for always being happy to receive excitable voice notes about 'what flower has bloomed today'. To Jim Sa Bom Nim from Clevedon Tang Soo Do for giving me ways to face the fear and do it anyway. To the Sweet Remembrance singing circle sisters for witnessing this year and receiving some of these poems fresh off the page. To my literary agent, Jane Graham-Maw for trying her best to find a home for this very unusual, wild and unwieldy collection. To Stephen Kane, for all the guidance and meditation suggestions to help me ground the energy of the project. And of course, to all the friends of the meadow on the cover of this book, in the pages of these poems, and forever in my heart. And finally to the Oak, the queen of the meadow, thanks for inviting me to spend a year with you.

About the Author

Natalie Fée is an award-winning environmental campaigner, singer-songwriter, author, nature poet and keynote speaker. Former founder of City to Sea, author of How to Save the World for Free, 'Do Good, Get Paid' and The Everyday Alchemist's Happiness Handbook, Natalie received an Honorary Doctorate of Science from the University of the West of England for her environmental work, won the Sunday Times Volvo Visionaries Award (2019) and has been named one of the UK's '50 New Radicals' by The Observer/Nesta (2018). She won the Sheila McKechnie Award for Environmental Justice in 2017 and was Bristol 24/7's Woman of the Year in 2018.

Her debut album, Daughter of Nature, features songs written during her year 'Under the Oak' and is available on all streaming platforms, as well as on her website.

www.nataliefee.com

nataliefee_ on instagram

Printed and bound in the United Kingdom
27/03/2026
02080149-0001